After having 1 *Reformation* by enjoyed, I knev publication copy of his biography on Martin Luther. Walker did not disappoint. His writing is crisp and flows very well. His prose is lucid and the text is extremely engaging. No doubt, this is an introductory work to the German Reformer and will be soaked up by those learning of Luther for the first time. However, as a quick refresher for the early Luther up to and including the Diet of Worms, this is a handy volume that gives much more than a dictionary entry can, even for more familiar readers. This is a very sympathetic portrait of the defiant defender of God's grace, but that should not be taken as a weakness. Reformed minded readers will revel in this account, and I suspect, will be hungry for more. I hope that Walker sharpens his pen and continues to give us the remainder of *Martin Luther: The Iron Pen*, and indeed, continues to edify the church with numerous more biographies of known and forgotten heroes of the faith. Highly recommended. Well done, Pastor Walker!

Dr. Theodore Zachariades
Sovereign Grace Baptist Church
Tullahoma, TN

MARTIN LUTHER

THE IRON PEN

MARTIN

LUTHER

THE IRON PEN

LUKE WALKER

They cannot defend themselves against me.

Martin Luther

WRATH AND GRACE PUBLISHING
COLUMBUS, GA

ACKNOWLEDGMENTS

While "the sun rises, and the sun goes down, and hastens to the place where it rises,"[1] time is not endless for mortal man. This volume, though small, has demanded great effort. Without the following people, this work would have lain forever dormant.

Thank you to my editing team, Brady Erickson, Nick Larson, Zach *Sneaky B* Larson, Franky Collazo, Carlos Gonzalez, Omri Miles, and Cali. Thank you Johan Henao for taking a chance on this wilderness penman. Thank you Theodore Zachariades for reading the work ahead of time and providing a very generous endorsement. Thank you to my sweet wife Angel for serving this project in many ways, and for taking care of our babies during this busy season. Thank you to the saints of Redeeming Cross for granting me the opportunity to throw myself into this effort, and thank you to Gottfried Caspari, my co-elder in the work of the gospel.

All thanks and praise to our triune God for redeeming wretched sinners like us and granting us the privilege of serving him in this life and for eternity.

---

[1] Ecclesiastes 1:5.

To Brady Erickson,
My brother and my friend

INTRODUCTION

As one not entirely unacquainted with the judges, I fancy Luther as the *Samson* of the Reformers. He knew as well how to throw down his foes as to boast over them in the Lord. His words will speak for themselves. He took up, not the jawbone of a donkey, but the feather of a goose and forged it into an implement of great power, a pen of iron. Ink from this pen continues to bleed into our own day; may it be that many pens continue to spring forth from it. Were a lone preacher equipped by this little volume to thunder the truths of God in the plain speech of the people, I shall be forever grateful unto God. The Lord Jesus Christ is worthy of such unassuming servants in dark hours of great need.

Luther, like Samson, was not a sinless man. Lest I be accused of hagiography, I hasten to remind my readers that this short biography is written in the not unbiblical spirit of Hebrews eleven. I intend to visit Luther's particular weaknesses in the next volume, Lord willing. For now, let us stand in wonder at what God did five centuries ago.

Luke Walker
October, 2017
Richfield, MN

MARTIN LUTHER
THE IRON PEN

As we take up the tale of the Protestant Reformation once again, the reader will recall that the winds have wafted the spirit of the martyr John Huss to the paradise of God, while they have scattered the seeds of truth across Bohemia. Years have washed over the Bohemian believers as they await the expected day of deliverance. Wars have raged, blood has been shed, peace has been realized, and all seems to indicate some sort of awakening at the very threshold. The world is hushed and stilled, poised for some great happening. It was now that Martinus Luther was born. "We may say without exaggeration that the Reformation was embodied in Martin Luther, that it lived in him as in no one else."[1]

It is with great joy that we come now to what may be termed *the sweet stuff*. All has led to this. Just as the weary journey makes the sight of the destination that much sweeter, the long sweep of the Dark Ages makes Luther's appearance as a breath of heavenly-fresh air.

[1] Thomas M. Lindsay, *A History of the Reformation* (Edinburgh: T. & T. Clark, 1956), 1.193.

EARLY LIFE

Luther was destined for hardship. He has been compared to the eagle—Huss forecasted him as such—
and even his youth bore this likeness:

> Let us mark the eagle and the bird of song,
> how dissimilar their rearing. The one is to
> spend its life in the groves, flitting from
> bough to bough, and enlivening the woods
> with its melody. Look what a warm nest it lies
> in; the thick branches cover it, and its dam
> sits brooding over it. How differently is the
> eaglet nursed! On yonder ledge, amid the
> naked crags, open to the lashing rain, and the
> pelting hail, and the stormy gust, are spread
> on the bare rock a few twigs. These are the
> nest of that bird which is to spend its after-
> life in soaring among the clouds, battling
> with the winds, and gazing upon the sun… It
> was thus [Luther] came to know that man
> lives not to enjoy, but to achieve.[1]

God seemed to hand-pick the Reformers, much
like the apostles, from the working classes of society.
Although Luther was raised in a tough, disciplinary

---

[1] James A. Wylie, *The History of Protestantism* (London: Cassell Petter & Galpin, 1899), 1.232.

home, he was also taught the doctrines of God's love. "The atmosphere of the family was that of the peasantry: rugged, rough, at times coarse, credulous, and devout."[1] While the scholastic leaders of the Church sank into sophist niceties and speculations, a form of living religion dwelt on in the homes of the people. Veiled as it was, it was imparted to the Reformers in their childhood homes. While mixed with much false and evil superstition, it is not perhaps untrue that the truths they encountered in their youth "were what Luther and Zwingli and Calvin wove into the Reformation creeds and expanded in Reformation sermons."[2]

Young Martin was a bright boy, sharp of wits, and the firstborn son of a miner. His father toiled and saved to send his promising son to law school. This would secure him prestige and a somewhat easier situation than his father had enjoyed in life. In this way "it fell to Martin Luder to advance his family's standing."[3] His family's standing *was* to be greatly advanced, though not in the manner envisioned by the patriarch. In a twist of fate, the son was destined to

[1] Ronald H. Bainton, *Here I Stand: A Life of Martin Luther* (Nashville: Abingdon Press, 1950), 10-11.
[2] Thomas M. Lindsay, *Luther and the German Reformation* (Edinburgh: T. & T. Clark, 1900), 14.
[3] R.C. Sproul and Stephen J. Nichols, *The Legacy of Luther* (Orlando: Reformation Trust, 2016), 16.

take up the career of the father, but the heir would
be a miner of *truth*.

As a teenage student, he went often to the library
at the University of Erfurt, such was his ravenous
hunger for books. Walking among these shelves, he
spies a strange volume and is pulled, as it were, within
the sphere of its orb. Such was its great weightiness.
Taking it and peering within, to his astonishment, it
was a full Bible. He saw that there were portions, yea,
entire books of Scripture that he had never heard of
before. He returned often to this lonely library to
devour the mysterious Book. The creative word of
the gospel first began to dawn upon Luther from the
pages of this very copy of God's word. "In that
Bible," ponders one, "the Reformation lay hid."[1]
Already "the old Luther was passing away, another
Luther was coming in his place."[2]

Not long after this, his life flashed before his
eyes. He was returning to school from visiting his
parents, and found himself in the center of a lightning storm. God's thunderbolts crashed around him
on every side. As the story goes, lightning struck the
ground right before him, and he fell on his face. He
was already shaken prior to the storm—shortly
before this time, one of his friends had suddenly

---

[1] J.H. Merle d'Aubigné, *History of the Reformation of the Sixteenth Century* (New
York: American Tract Society, 1849), 1.157.
[2] Wylie, *History*, 1.233.

died. Confronted by the fiery arrows of God, he thinks to himself: *This is it! It is now that I will stand before God.* He begged God for mercy—in fact, he begged a mediator, Saint Anne[1]—and swore that, if spared, he would become a monk.

The storm passed. He stood on his feet and made his way back to town. The vow has been made; it cannot be broken. The promising scholar gathers his friends for a dinner and, as the night grows long, he finally breaks the heart-wrenching news to them. That very night, a monk he would become. He kissed the world goodbye; all was loss.

THE MONK

Monastic life was considered the height of medieval holiness. In the early ages of the Church there were martyrs by the thousands. The bloodshed ceased with Constantine's conversion, but some believers still desired the crown of martyrdom. Thus, they fashioned a martyrdom of their own make: the slow martyrdom of hermit life. A tale or two will help illustrate these strange beginnings.

These *witnesses* dwelt in solitary nomadism in the wilderness. The books tell of one whose hair and

---

[1] *Grandmother of God,* as they might have it. Anne was supposed to be Mary's mother.

beard grew to such extremes that a shepherd mistook him for a wolf and nearly killed him, "till he discovered his error, and then worshiped the hermit as a saint."[1] Another dined every night with his only companion in life, a female *lupus*.[2] Some of these discerning souls swore to high heaven that they had seen animals repent and believe. Their communion with the lower creatures was remarkable; one is said to have crossed the Nile standing on the backs of crocodiles.[3] As the years rolled by, the matter was, shall we say, *elevated*. Pillar saints lived in deserts atop columns for decades at a stretch. Pillars of truth, no doubt!

In the Middle Ages, communal monasteries multiply. As one tale goes, St. Brandon stumbled upon a cloister of twenty-four monks in his ocean wanderings. He was impressed by their strict, godly conduct and soon learned that these pious souls had not said a word to one another in eighty years. The astonished pilgrim "wept for joy" at this exceeding holiness.[4] The example may well serve to show how *dumb* the matter had become.

Luther, threatened with death and judgment, does the obvious thing and flees to the holy refuge

---

[1] Philip Schaff, *History of the Christian Church* (New York: Charles Scribner's Sons, 1916), 3.167.

[2] Ibid., 3.168.

[3] Ibid., 3.197.

[4] Ibid., 5.1.319-20.

of the monastery. With broken heart over his great love for learning, he vanished into the night. It was not to be his last disappearance.

But he was not a Christian yet. We might say he was a medieval Christian; "however, the mysterious motions of *regeneration* had not been worked on his heart."[1] He was, however, deeply sincere in these efforts. He *meant* to win heaven by the monastery. "They were the rigorists, heroic athletes, seeking to take heaven by force."[2] He did all the chores. He wore out his confessors. "Every sin in order to be absolved was to be confessed. Therefore the soul must be searched and the memory ransacked and the motives probed."[3] One such confessor said, "Man, God is not angry with you. You are angry with God."[4] We think at this juncture that both were true, for the wrath of God yet abode on the young man.

His sincerity must be born in mind. While he was hilarious and giftedly witty, when it came to the things of God he was as serious as death. "Never did the Romish church possess a more pious monk."[5] He says of himself, "If ever a monk got to heaven by monkery, I would have gotten there."[6] But as he

---

[1] Luke Walker, *Olaudah Equiano: The Interesting Man* (Columbus: Wrath and Grace, 2017), 12.
[2] Bainton, *Here I Stand*, 29.
[3] Ibid., 39.
[4] Ibid.
[5] d'Aubigné, *History*, 1.168.
[6] Schaff, *History*, 6.116.

sought the Lord in these ways he was left empty. He was sunken into the lowest depths of convictions, even depression. "The word he used was *Anfechtung*, for which there is no English equivalent... It is all the doubt, turmoil, pang, tremor, panic, despair, desolation, and desperation which invade the spirit of man."[1]

The path he was on did not make him right with God, and it was not changing his heart. In fact, he only saw more of his sin than ever and was plunged into darkness and doubt. It seems that the Mosaic tutor, though under a different form, was driving the medieval monk to despair of himself. "To be able to deliver his age from the miserable superstitions under which it grew, it was necessary for him first to feel their weight. To drain the cup, he must drink it to the very dregs."[2] He passed through what the Medieval church considered to be the highest form of godliness and saw he had been sold a bill of goods. And yet, in the valley God was preparing his chosen instrument, sharpening it for its work. The champion was being clad unawares.[3]

"In one word, Luther passed through the experience of Paul. He understood him better than any

[1] Bainton, *Here I Stand*, 26.

[2] d'Aubigné, *History*, 1.166.

[3] "The great revolt against the medieval Church arose from a desperate attempt to follow the way by her prescribed." Bainton, *Here I Stand*, 20.

medieval schoolman or ancient father."[1] Just as Paul became a public spectacle of God's mercy, Luther was a sort of *representative* in these things. "It is not Luther alone whose cries we hear. Christendom is groaning in Luther, and travailing in pain to be delivered."[2] What he came to was this: "The highest degree of wisdom attained by ambitious minds, or by souls bursting with the desire of perfection, has been to despair of themselves."[3] It is not a sin here and there that must be confessed. "The whole nature of man needs to be changed,"[4] because the whole nature of man is corrupted. It is not a matter of making bad men good; it must needs be the making of dead men live.

One verse haunted him in his reading of Scripture. It was Romans 1:17, and especially the last phrase: *the just shall live by faith.* "These words hunted Luther's soul."[5] When he finally understood the divine meaning, the verse was transformed for him into the gate of heaven. He knew himself, having studied law, that he was condemned. How could God's bare righteousness be good news for sinners? "I could not endure those words—the righteousness of God. I had no love for that holy and just God who

---

[1] Schaff, *History*, 6.125.

[2] Wylie, *History*, 1.238.1

[3] d'Aubigné, *History*, 1.217.

[4] Bainton, *Here I Stand*, 41.

[5] d'Aubigné, *History*, 1.197.

punishes sinners. I was filled with secret anger against him."[1] But that holy and just God began to break in upon Luther's soul.

Paul had spoken of a righteousness that God gives to the sinner by faith, which counts the sinner righteous before him.[2] Luther says, "Then I felt born again like a new man; I entered through the open doors into the very paradise of God... In very truth, this language of St. Paul was to me the true gate of paradise."[3] It was now that "the whole of Scripture took on a new meaning."[4] Faith unites the sinner to Christ, who says to the trusting soul:

> *For I am thine and thou art mine,*
> *And where I am our lives entwine.*[5]

I wonder, has my reader passed through this experience? You must! Or you must forever despair of your own salvation.

The vicar general of the Augustinian monasteries was named Staupitz. He was a good man, but of a much gentler specimen than Luther. He was not ready for that rough age the Reformation was to be.

---

[1] Ibid., 1.198.
[2] "Light broke at last through the examination of exact shades of meaning in the Greek language." Bainton, *Here I Stand*, 50.
[3] d'Aubigné, *History*, 1.199.
[4] Baintin, *Here I Stand*, 51.
[5] Ibid., 53.

And yet in his own way he lays claims to all the labors of Luther. "If it had not been for Staupitz," said the Reformer, "I should have sunk in hell."[1] He is not unlike the anonymous preacher who was given the privilege of seeing young Charles Spurgeon's conversion. Won't that be a tale to tell!

Staupitz had come to Luther one day and said, "We cannot understand God out of Jesus Christ."[2] How often we need this reminder! For there is nothing but wrath and judgment for the exposed sinner outside of Christ; but in him the love of God is made manifest. The full knowledge of God is in Jesus Christ. When this dawned upon the convicted monk, "all the passages of Scripture that used to alarm him seemed now to run to him from every part, to smile and sport around him."[3] In this way, Luther despaired of his own works and was converted to a living faith.

But his training was not complete. He did not appear in the fullness of knowledge, as Wycliffe appeared to do so long before him. "Luther became enlightened only by degrees."[4] The monastery had business in Rome and sent Brother Martin to take the journey. "Staupitz thought this a fine occasion

---

[1] Ibid., 38.
[2] d'Aubigné, *History*, 1.179.
[3] Ibid., 1.177.
[4] Ibid., 1.209.

for Luther to be cured of his *Anfechtungen*."[1] To be sure!

He walked by foot from Germany to Rome, and when the city came into view he exclaimed, "Holy Rome, I salute thee!" The loyalty he still felt gives his eventual separation from Rome a genuine credibility, and his overthrow of it a significant power. When he left Rome a few weeks later, the common sentiment was in his mouth: "If there is a hell, Rome is built over it."[2] Makiavelli[3] had said, "The strongest symptom of the approaching ruin of Christianity is that the nearer people get to the capital of Christendom, the less Christian spirit is found in them."[4] Luther must learn this firsthand.

He went through all the motions; he saw all the relics. Apparently, the stairway of Pilate had been transferred from one holy city to the other. He climbed the steps doing the prescribed penance to release his grandfather from purgatory. He even "regretted that his own father and mother were not yet dead and in purgatory so that he might confer on them so signal a favor."[5] It was a fine way of setting aside the commandment of God for the sake of their tradition!

---

[1] Nichols, *Legacy*, 18.
[2] d'Aubigné, *History*, 1.196.
[3] The real one, not 2Pac.
[4] d'Aubigné, *History*, 1.196.
[5] Bainton, *Here I Stand*, 35.

And yet, in the midst of these motions, that blessed verse seemed to shout at his soul. "At every step the word of Scripture sounded as a significant protest in his ear: 'The just shall live by faith.'"[1] When he reached the top, the vendors assured him of the promised grace, to which he said, "Who knows whether it is so?"[2] We think Luther knew by now that it was not so.

> This powerful text has a mysterious influence on the life of Luther. It was a *creative* sentence both for the reformer and for the Reform- ation… This great doctrine of salvation pro- ceeding from God and not from man, was not only the power of God to save Luther's soul; it became in a still greater degree the power of God to reform the Church:—an effectual weapon wielded by the apostles,— a weapon too long neglected, but taken at last, in its primitive brightness, from the arsenal of the omnipotent God.[3]

"When he turned his back on Rome, he turned his face toward the Bible. The Bible henceforward was

---

[1] Schaff, *History*, 6.129.
[2] Bainton, *Here I Stand*, 35.
[3] d'Aubigné, *History*, 1.198.

to be to Luther the true city of God."[1] Let us see how his citizenship fares in this heavenly metropolis.

THE PASTOR-SCHOLAR

Upon his return, a new university was being constructed not far from him, in Wittenberg. Frederick the Wise, Elector of Saxony, the prince ruler, had great hopes for this new school. He "declared that he and his people would look to that school as to an oracle. At that time, he had little thought in how remarkable a manner this language would be verified."[2] Luther was recommended and called to become one of his professors.

He commenced with teaching philosophy, but eventually was granted the privilege—the burning desire which ate away at his soul—to teach Scripture. He began expositing the Bible to his students. In the classroom, Luther spoke like someone who came from a different realm. He cracked open books of the Bible that had laid long dormant. "This entirely new method of expounding the truth made a great noise."[3] Expositing the Psalms, he came to further understand the cross. "Christ too," he realized, "had

---

[1] Wylie, *History*, 1.255.
[2] d'Aubigné, *History*, 1.184.
[3] Ibid., 1.187.

Anfechtungen."[1] But why would the perfect Son of God suffer the wrath of God? It was in our place that he did so. "He was crushed for our iniquities."[2] This was as life to the dead for Luther, a further awakening.

It was now that he was called to the pulpit. An old wooden church in Wittenberg was to be the springtime flower of his mighty preaching ministry. "This building," says one, not unremarkably, "may well be compared to the stable in which Christ was born. It was in this wretched enclosure that God willed, so to speak, that his well-beloved Son should be born a second time."[3]

Luther was a mouthpiece of powerful eloquence, a preacher of the finest mint. "He affected his hearers' minds in a surprising manner, and carried them like a torrent wherever he pleased."[4] He was a master of his native tongue and had no equal in all of Germany in the spoken, living speech of the people. "In classical culture, he never attained to the height of Erasmus or Melanchthon, or Calvin and Beza, but in original thought and in the mastery of his own mother tongue he was unrivaled."[5]

---

[1] Bainton, *Here I Stand*, 46.
[2] Isaiah 53:5.
[3] Myconius, quoted in d'Aubigné, *History*, 1.188.
[4] Ibid.
[5] Schaff, *History*, 6.110.

As to the content of his preaching, let us hear it in his own words. "All sermons," he says, "and all instructions that do not set Jesus Christ before us, and teach us to know him, cannot be the daily bread and the nourishment of our souls."[1] This was the live nerve of Luther's pulpit. In a day in which forgiveness required the hierarchy of the church, he says, "If a simple Christian says to you, God pardons sins in the name of Jesus Christ, and you receive this word with firm faith, as if God himself were talking to you, you are absolved."[2] Such ran the doctrine of Martinus Luther, Augustinian monk.[3]

He was finally called to become a Doctor of Divinity at Wittenberg. It was now that he became a sworn defendant of Scripture; he was here equipped to become the Reformer he was destined to be. He resisted the call to the doctorate with all his might. It was only after his superiors pleaded greatly with him that he finally resigned the matter to God and obeyed. This became a bulwark to him. He moved through the spheres of his life with the greatest ease of conscience because he could say along every step of the way that he did not seek his own glory. It was the work of God to spread his tent abroad. This was God's business.

---

[1] d'Aubigné, *History*, 1.321-22.

[2] Ibid., 1.324.

[3] "Men were astonished that they had not earlier acknowledged truths that appeared to evident in his mouth." Ibid., 1.209.

On that memorable day, he was made the armed champion of the Bible. He threw down the scholastic rulers of the time: Aquinas and *the Philosopher* himself, Aristotle. "I understand him better than St. Thomas or Duns Scotus," he later said.[1] Not all things did he oppose in the medieval scholastics, but those which most pressed his own day with grave error:

> If I profess with the loudest voice and clearest exposition every portion of the truth of God except precisely that little point which the world and the devil are at that moment attacking, I am not confessing Christ, however boldly I may be professing Christ. Where the battle rages, there the loyalty of the soldier is proved.[2]

The Lombardian schoolmen could not stand before the living word of God. It *sentenced* their speculations to death. "Let them read this book," said Luther, "and then let them say whether our theology is new. But this is not a new book."[3]

He later reflected, in shocking terms:

---

[1] Martin Luther, *Three Treatises* (Minneapolis: Fortress Press, 1990), 93-4.
[2] Sproul and Nichols, *Legacy*, 32.
[3] d'Aubigné, *History*, 1.213.

He who undertakes any thing without a divine call, seeks his own glory. But I, Doctor Martin Luther, was forced to become a doctor. Popery desired to stop me in the performance of my duty: but you see what has happened to it, and worse things still will befall it. They cannot defend themselves against me. I am determined, in God's name, to tread upon the lions, to trample dragons and serpents under foot. This will begin during my life, and will be accomplished after my death.[1]

It was at this period, 1516, when "Luther awakened many drowsy souls by his words. Hence this year has been named the morning star of the gospel day."[2] It would appear that our old friends Wycliffe and Huss are back. And now the eagle will fly, now the swan will sing.

1517

The *indulgent* Pope Leo needs money, and lots of it. He not only needs it to build Saint Peter's cathedral in Rome, but he needs to cover his massive expen-

---

[1] Ibid., 1.205.
[2] Ibid., 1.222.

ditures on the finest of luxuries, "as elegant and as indolent as a Persian cat" was he.[1] He preferred the sport of the field to the custom of the holy court. "He wore long hunting boots which impeded the kissing of his toe."[2] His privy council no doubt *nailed* him for it. Luther was later to compare the booted outdoorsman to Nimrod the mighty: "The papacy is The Grand Hunting of the Bishop of Rome."[3]

How is Leo going to raise the much-needed funds? He set a price on the well sought archbishopric of Maintz for its aspirant, Albert of Brandenberg. "He was informed that the pope demanded twelve thousand ducats for the twelve apostles. Albert offered seven thousand for the seven deadly sins. They compromised on ten thousand, presumably not for the Ten Commandments."[4] The holy price was paid and Albert was in turn allowed to raise money for reimbursement. What course shall he pursue? Ah! The time-tested recourse of Rome: "Let's sell heaven." A precious commodity, and highly sought by the poor of Germany. It was specifically the superabundant merits of the saints that were offered, for, according to their doctrine, "goodness can be pooled."[5] What a

---

[1] Bainton, *Here I Stand*, 61.

[2] Ibid.

[3] Luther, *Three Treatises*, 125.

[4] Bainton, *Here I Stand*, 62.

[5] Ibid., 31.

rotten cesspool of filth *all our righteous deeds* would make, who can tell? But I digress.

Indulgences were first offered in the Crusades, and later through the viewing of relics. How many skulls and bones of the saints Rome possessed, one may well wonder. They had even secured one of the coins that Judas received for betraying Christ. "Its value had greatly increased, for now it was able to confer an indulgence of fourteen hundred years."[1] The worth of such relics was great, for "they were the bingo of the sixteenth century."[2]

Leo and Albert begin to reap quite the harvest from this endeavor. A man named Tetzel was commissioned to sell these indulgences in Germany. He was an infamous man; he almost received the death penalty prior to becoming a Dominican monk and the holy herald of dear Mother Church. They sent him to sell heaven out of thin air to the poor of Germany. Who hasn't heard his famous mantra?

> *When a coin in the coffer rings,*
> *The soul from purgatory springs.*

At this time "one half of Christendom reveled in their sin, because they were wealthy, and the other half groaned under self-inflected mortifications be-

---

[1] Ibid., 32.
[2] Ibid., 58.

cause they were poor."[1] Allow me to indulge my readers with a choice anecdote, and one which, I trust, shall not fail to richly reward the attention of the hearer:

> A Saxon nobleman, who had heard Tetzel at Leipsic, was much displeased by his false-hoods. Approaching the monk, he asked him if he had the power of pardoning sins that men have an intention of committing. "Most assuredly," replied Tetzel, "I have received full powers from his holiness for that pur-pose."—"Well, then," answered the knight, "I am desirous of taking a slight revenge on one of my enemies, without endangering his life. I will give you ten crowns if you will give me a letter of indulgence that shall fully jus-tify me." Tetzel made some objections; they came however to an arrangement by the aid of thirty crowns. The monk quitted Leipsic shortly after. The nobleman and his atten-dants lay in wait for him in a wood between Jüterbock and Treblin; they fell upon him, gave him a slight beating, and took away the well-stored indulgence-chest the inquisitor was carrying with him. Tetzel made a violent

---

[1] Wylie, *History*, 1.242.

outcry, and carried his complaint before the courts. But the nobleman showed the letter which Tetzel had signed himself, and which exempted him beforehand from every penalty. Duke George, whom this action had at first exceedingly exasperated, no sooner read the document than he ordered the accused to be acquitted.[1]

The shrewd Saxon was not alone in his displeasure with the sales. The people reasoned that, if the pope has power to give this grace, "Why does not the pope deliver at once all the souls from purgatory by his holy charity on account of their great wretchedness, since you deliver so many for love of perishable money and the Cathedral of Saint Peter?"[2] Searing question. "The pope would do better," says Luther, "to give away everything without charge."[3] If money is the object, let him sell St. Peter's. This was the common sentiment. These Romish men were prosperity preachers—or rather, popesperity preachers, to *coin* a phrase. Tetzel closed his sermons with the customary shout of, "Bring—bring—bring!"[4] "Pay! Pay! That is the head, belly,

---

[1] d'Aubigné, *History*, 1.254.

[2] Ibid., 1.254-55.

[3] Bainton, *Here I Stand*, 68.

[4] d'Aubigné, *History*, 1.243.

tail, and all the contents of their sermons."[1] Such was their reckless greed that even the following statement was vomited from the dungeon of Tetzel's filthy breast: "Even if any one (which is doubtless impossible) had offered violence to the blessed Virgin Mary, mother of God, let him pay—only let him pay well, and all will be forgiven him."[2]

How did Luther become engaged in this battle? He certainly did not seek it out for himself. He had critiqued indulgences from the pulpit before, to the chagrin of the elector. In fact, Tetzel was forbidden from entering the realm of Wittenberg because he would encroach on the indulgences offered by Frederick, the great All Saints Day lottery. But he approached as near to Wittenberg as he could. Dangerous ground! For "Tetzel was now almost within earshot of the Reformer."[3] A friend came and told him, "That Tetzel is making a lot of noise about the indulgences." "If God permits," returned Luther, "I will make a hole in his drum."[4]

This battle was brought to Luther in the faithfulness of his duty. "He was a priest responsible for the eternal welfare of his parishioners."[5] As a priest, he was in the custom of hearing the confes-

---

[1] Ibid., 1.255.
[2] Ibid., 1.241.
[3] Wylie, *History*, 1.261.
[4] d'Aubigné, *History*, 1.260.
[5] Bainton, *Here I Stand*, 60.

sions of the people. He noticed that many were
confessing wild sins, to which he replied, that they
must also repent for these sins. "Well, Father
Martin" say the lambs, "we received these indulgences which clear us." They had come "with the
most amazing concessions."[1] And so it came about
that it was the humble call of pastoral duty which
thrust Martin Luther into the fray. Rome brought the
fight to him; they knocked on the wrong door.

We are going to step, it may be, just a bit outside
the realm of strict history to quote a relevant passage
at length. "It is a dream of the elector's, the essence
of which is no doubt true, although some circum-
stances may have been added by those who related
it."[2] It was put down by Spalatin:

> On the morning of the 31st of October, 1517, the
> elector said to Duke John, "Brother, I must tell you a
> dream which I had last night, and the meaning of
> which I should like much to know. It is so deeply im-
> pressed on my mind, that I will never forget it, were I
> to live a thousand years. For I dreamed it thrice, and
> each time with new circumstances."
>
> Duke John: "Is it a good or a bad dream?"
>
> The Elector: "I know not; God knows."
>
> Duke John: "Don't be uneasy at it; but be so good
> as to tell it to me."

---

[1] Ibid., 62.
[2] d'Aubigné, *History*, 1.265.

The Elector: "Having gone to bed last night, fatigued and out of spirits, I fell asleep shortly after my prayer, and slept calmly for about two hours and a half; I then awoke, and continued awake to midnight, all sorts of thoughts passing through my mind. Among other things, I thought how I was to observe the Feast of All Saints. I prayed for the poor souls in purgatory; and supplicated God to guide me, my counsels, and my people according to truth. I again fell asleep, and then dreamed that Almighty God sent me a monk, who was a true son of the Apostle Paul. All the saints accompanied him by order of God, in order to bear testimony before me, and to declare that he did not come to contrive any plot, but that all that he did was according to the will of God. They asked me to have the goodness graciously to permit him to write something on the door of the church of the Castle of Wittemberg. This I granted through my chancellor. Thereupon the monk went to the church, and began to write in such large characters that I could read the writing at Schweinitz. The pen which he used was so large that its end reached as far as Rome, where it pierced the ears of a lion that was crouching there, and caused the triple crown upon the head of the Pope to shake. All the cardinals and princes, running hastily up, tried to prevent it from falling. You and I, brother, wished also to assist, and I stretched out my arm;— but at this moment I awoke, with my arm in the air, quite amazed, and very much enraged at the monk for not managing his pen better. I recollected myself a little; it was only a dream.

"I was still half asleep, and once more closed my eyes. The dream returned. The lion, still annoyed by the pen, began to roar with all his might, so much so that the whole city of Rome, and all the States of the Holy Empire, ran to see what the matter was. The Pope requested them to oppose this monk, and applied particularly to me, on account of his being in my country. I again awoke, repeated the Lord's prayer, entreated God to preserve his Holiness, and once more fell asleep.

"Then I dreamed that all the princes of the Empire, and we among them, hastened to Rome, and strove, one after another, to break the pen; but the more we tried the stiffer it became, sounding as if it had been made of iron. We at length desisted. I then asked the monk (for I was sometimes at Rome, and sometimes at Wittemberg) where he got this pen, and why it was so strong. 'The pen,' replied he, 'belonged to an old goose of Bohemia, a hundred years old. I got it from one of my old schoolmasters. As to its strength, it is owing to the impossibility of depriving it of its pith or marrow; and I am quite astonished at it myself.' Suddenly I heard a loud noise—a large number of other pens had sprung out of the long pen of the monk. I awoke a third time: it was daylight."

Duke John: "Chancellor, what is your opinion? Would we had a Joseph, or a Daniel, enlightened by God!"

Chancellor: "Your highness knows the common proverb, that the dreams of young girls, learned men, and great lords have usually some hidden meaning. The meaning of this dream, however, we shall not be able to know for some time—not till the things to which it relates have taken place. Wherefore, leave the accomplishment to God, and place it fully in his hand."

Duke John: "I am of your opinion, Chancellor; 'tis not fit for us to annoy ourselves in attempting to discover the meaning. God will overrule all for his glory."

Elector: "May our faithful God do so; yet I shall never forget this dream. I have, indeed, thought of an interpretation, but I keep it to myself. Time, perhaps, will show if I have been a good diviner."

So passed the morning of October 31, 1517, in the royal castle of Schweinitz… The elector has hardly made an end of telling his dream when the monk comes with his hammer to interpret it.[1]

"We are now returning," says the historian, "entirely to the domain of history."[2] That very morning Luther walked up to the Castle church and nailed a weighty document to the door, his famed Ninety-Five Theses. They only numbered 95, but (let the reader understand) he kept it *100*.

He nailed them up and summoned a discussion on the morrow, All Saints Day. Such matters were commonly handled this way. No one showed up. The Theses did not even condemn indulgences *as such*, but rather the manner of their administration. "A mad papist" is what he later calls himself.[3] And yet, "the ninety-five affirmations are crisp, bold, unqualified."[4] He had posted the theses in full belief

[1] Wylie, *History*, 1.263-66; d'Aubigné, *History*, 1.265-67.

[2] d'Aubigné, *History*, 1.267.

[3] *Papista insanissimus.* Schaff, *History*, 6.158.

[4] Bainton, *Here I Stand*, 66.

that, had the pope known the manner of these sales, he would have shut it down. Alas! How disappointed Luther was in his expectation! Little did he know that the sound of his hammer would "resound through-out Christendom, and centuries after he had gone to his grave, would be sending back their echoes in the fall of hierarchies."[1]

The Ninety-Five Theses went absolutely viral. The printing press was the internet of that day. "Now was seen the power of that instrumentality which God had prepared beforehand for this emergency—the printing-press."[2] The document flew through Germany. The people were already upset; Luther's pen gave them a voice. It channeled the popular sentiment. It was the perfect time for the match to be struck. All was in order for a fiery advancement of truth. The indulgences were not the cause of the Reformation—the thing itself was long in coming—but they were the *occasion* of it. For, as in the days of old, the Lord was seeking an opportunity against them.[3]

The self-styled *mad papist* had already come to believe in the free grace of God, and the essence of the 95 Theses breathes that. He had not yet worked out the truths he was putting on paper; indeed, his

---

[1] Wylie, *History*, 1.266.
[2] Ibid..
[3] Judges 14:4.

pen taught him wonderful things. Rome, however, certainly picked up what he was laying down. They saw that if the implications were traced out, their own power would be threatened by it. A real nightmare had appeared to them on that All Hallows Eve. Unsuspectingly, he had struck at the root. "Him whom we have so long expected is come at last," said one, "and he will show the monks a trick or two!"[1] Even Emperor Maximillian said, "He will play the monks a pretty game."[2] Luther alone seemed to be unaware of the career he had launched upon.

"These theses spread with the rapidity of lightning…as if the very angels had been their messengers… No one can believe the noise they made… God gave them wings."[3] "The movement is fairly launched. It is speeding on, it grows not by weeks only, but by hours and moments."[4] It was pandemonium. They were printed out and taken by foot or horseback with, it seems, more swiftness even than our modern tweet is capable of. "In a month they had made the tour of Europe."[5]

The storm of reform was long gathering, but it was given to Luther to blow a hole in the thing. He had an explosive ministry. The theses broke the spell

---

[1] Dr. Flack, quoted in d'Aubigné, *History*, 1.281.

[2] Ibid., 1.282.

[3] Ibid., 1.278.

[4] Wylie, *History*, 1.263.

[5] d'Aubigné, *History*, 1.267.

that had opened to Rome all the wealth of Europe. Luther was more shocked than anybody at how they fared. "I entered into this controversy," he says, "without any definite plan, without knowledge or inclination; I was quite taken unawares, and I call God, the searcher of hearts, to witness."[1] This was not Luther's movement, it was God's.

Later, he says, "God does not guide me, he pushes me forward, he carries me away. I am not master of myself. I desire to live in repose; but I am thrown into the midst of tumults and revolutions."[2] It was God's truth in the man that must find a way out; he was unable to arrest it. He gained strength by the hour. "The sermons written out by request on Monday do not correspond to the notes taken by hearers on Sunday. Ideas were so churning within him that new butter always come out of the vat."[3] His mind was a machine, the heat of which melted the weak thoughts of his foes. And thus it was said to them, "There you are, like butter in sunshine."[4]

---

[1] Ibid., 1.275.

[2] Ibid., 2.27.

[3] Bainton, *Here I Stand*, 75.

[4] *Luther's Works* (Minneapolis: Fortress Press, 1958), 40.252.

1518

These blows of God's new champion did not fail to send back echoes of opposition. At this period, Luther entered into single combat with Roman champions and, in the words of old Drinian, "unhorsed many knights."[1] He was made for this. "Luther was a born fighter, and waxed stronger and stronger in battle."[2] He wrote in a letter, "I am ready for peace and for war: but I prefer peace."[3] He was God's ready-man. "In attacking their doctrine, we take the goose by the neck. Everything depends on the Word, which the pope has taken from us and falsified."[4] In later days, he boasted as one who takes off his armor: "I have vanquished the Pope, because my doctrine is of God and his is of the devil."[5]

Tetzel must answer Luther. He wrote theses of his own in response. The contrast between the men is worthy of note:

One thing strikes us, as we read Tetzel's reply—the difference between the German

---

[1] C.S. Lewis, *The Voyage of the "Dawn Treader"* (New York: Macmillan Publishing Company, 1970), 17.

[2] Schaff, *History*, 6.143.

[3] d'Aubigné, *History*, 1.318.

[4] Ibid., 1.273.

[5] Ibid.

employed by him and Luther. One might say they were several ages apart. A foreigner, in particular, sometimes finds it difficult to understand Tetzel, while Luther's language is almost entirely that of our own days. A comparison of the writings is sufficient to show that Luther is the creator of the German language.[1]

Tetzel's real play was to take Luther's theses and burn them. "He knew better," said Luther, "how to do this than to maintain theses."[2] He would have gladly added the author himself to the fire, which was the purpose of his mind throughout the combat. But it was not to be; Luther came to finish what the ashes of Huss had begun.

He was now summoned before a papal legate named Cajetan to recant his errors. He was instructed to lay on his face before the popish authority; when told to stand, he was to kneel. All Cajetan wanted to hear—how simple!—was six letters, *revoco*. Luther reckoned those six letters better weighed than counted. He did not revoke, but instead reasoned. "Luther answered that he had not made the arduous journey to Augsburg to do what he could have done quite as well at Wittenberg. He would like to be

---

[1] Ibid., 1.291.

[2] Ibid., 1.302.

instructed as to his errors."[1] The poor monk drew the papal legate into a contest, and came out the champion. "Luther wrote home that the cardinal was no more fitted to handle the case than an ass to play on a harp."[2] Leo had sent Cajetan to grab Luther, not to contend with him. He was to secure a recantation, or arrest and bring him to Rome.[3] At this hour, Leo compared him to "a child of the evil one."[4] These words had apparently eluded his memory when he later called Luther his dear son.[5]

On the way, the people cheered him on, but they mixed their encouragements with warnings. "Dear brother, in Augsburg you will meet with Italians, who are learned men, but more likely to burn you than to answer you."[6] The single monk responded in his customary wit: "My wife and my children are well provided for; my field, my houses, my goods are in order. They have already destroyed my honor and my reputation. One single thing remains; it is my wretched body. Let them take it... As for my soul, they cannot take that."[7]

This was a holy confidence that is not often seen among men. Listen to this! "If [God] maintains his

[1] Bainton, Here I Stand, 82.

[2] Ibid., 84.

[3] Ibid., 80.

[4] d'Aubigné, History, 1.354.

[5] Lindsay, History, 1.234.

[6] Wylie, History, 1.275.

[7] d'Aubigné, History, 1.366.

cause, mine is maintained; but if he does not maintain it, of a truth it is not I who can maintain it, and it is he who will bear the dishonour."[1] It was a rare conjunction of heavenly lights; faith-filled boldness and sincere humility coalesce in Luther. God was pleased, for he added his strong blessing to the cause.

He escaped Augsburg untouched. He was led before dawn to a side gate and rode off into the free air, for only now did he realize that a sword had been hanging over his head. He returned to Wittenberg, awaiting the next blow. "I am expecting the curses of Rome any day. I have everything in readiness. When they come, I am girded like Abraham to go I know not where, but sure of this, that God is everywhere."[2] He began to cast his gaze around if perhaps he might escape to another quarter of Christendom. Even Frederick, for a moment, told him to leave. His eyes dart here and there, and pause upon France.[3] The student of history wonders, what might Luther in Paris have been? It would have been something, but it was not God's will. Another champion, most well beloved and genius, was to come from that region at his appointed time in the drama now unfolding before us.

---

[1] Ibid., 1.368.
[2] Bainton, *Here I Stand*, 88.
[3] d'Aubigné, *History*, 1.416.

"In another two hours he would have left had not a letter come from Spalatin saying that the prince wished him to stay."[1] Wittenberg reached a truce with Rome. Luther was not excommunicated—not yet! The terms were simple: *You don't talk about it, we don't talk about it.* But it was not meant to be.

1519

The truce was broken, but not by Luther. In these Middle Ages—for Luther, it must be remembered, is a Medieval man—scholastics took great pride in their learning and looked upon academic debates like knights going to contest to win honor. One such man, Dr. Johann Eck, was "the most illustrious of goosequill gladiators and braggadocios."[2] Here was a Johann who could bring forth both wrath and grace with his fine speeches. He thought he had "the best words,"[3] and could not resist attacking the new challenger. It was he who broke the truce. This was the worst thing that could happen to Rome, for the best words were Luther's. His voice was a very trumpet.

---

[1] Bainton, *Here I Stand*, 89.

[2] d'Aubigné, *History*, 2.34.

[3] Pres. Trump. https://www.washingtonpost.com/video/national/trump-i-have-the-best-words/2017/04/05/53a9ae4a-19fd-11e7-8598-9a99da559f9e_video.html?utm_term=.3a74bb9a9f1f

The white-belted Johann challenged him to a Jiu Jitsu of the mind. Rome was not extraordinarily keen on putting their hundreds of years of victories to a single combat, especially with *that guy*. Cajetan had said, "I will no longer dispute with that beast, for it has deep eyes and wonderful speculations in its head."[1] It was yet to be seen the *beast* Luther would become in the cause of truth. "Eck is fomenting new wars against me. He may yet drive me to a serious attack upon the Romanists. So far I have been merely trifling."[2] And so, a debate was arranged in Leipsic.

His preparations drove him into deeper learning. "I am studying the papal decretals for my debate," he wrote to Spalatin. "I whisper this in your ear, 'I do not know whether the pope is Antichrist or his apostle, so does he in his decretals corrupt and crucify Christ, that is, the truth.'"[3] In fact Luther was not only to land upon this conclusion; he was to advance it beyond the thoughts of his predecessors, Wycliffe and Huss. "Whereas they identified particular popes, because of their evil lives, with Antichrist, Luther held that every pope was Antichrist even though personally exemplary, because Antichrist is collective: an institution, the papacy, a system which corrupts the truth of Christ."[4] This discovery fused a

---

[1] d'Aubigné, *History*, 1.397.
[2] Bainton, *Here I Stand*, 98.
[3] Ibid.
[4] Ibid., 99.

fresh vitality into his work, "for the doom of Antichrist was sure."[1] He was fighting a defeated foe; he was carrying out God's decree.

At this time, the University of Wittenberg called for new professors. The study of the ancient languages was flourishing and a Greek scholar was needed. Frederick received a recommendation for a promising young student named Schwartzert, who was "enjoying already a European reputation."[2] He was appointed to be professor of Greek at Wittenberg. He was a midget of a man in his twenty first year, and none too dashing, if pictures tell truth. When he arrived, the professors sniffed at him. But when he gave his first lecture, Luther called him "a *man*."[3] His lecture halls were filled, not only with students, but with professors. Of course, you know him by the Greek translation of his name, *Melanchthon*.

The young scholar was destined to be Luther's yoke-fellow. A contemporary remarked, "To look at Melanchthon you would say he was a mere boy; but in understanding, learning, and talent, he was a giant, and I cannot comprehend how such heights of wisdom and genius can be found in so small a body."[4] When asked what he thought the apostle Paul looked

---

[1] Ibid., 101.
[2] Ibid., 95.
[3] d'Aubigné, *History*, 1.360. Emphasis mine.
[4] Ibid., 2.47.

like, Luther replied, "I think he was a scrawny shrimp like Melanchthon."[1]

Together, they were stick up kids who robbed Rome of its goods. "These two were the compliment the one of the other; united, they formed a complete Reformer... It doubled the working powers of each for both to draw the same yoke."[2] "They were not so much twain as one; they made up between them the perfect agent for the times and for the work."[3] Luther said, "I am the rough woodsman, who has to prepare the way and smooth the road. But Philip advances quietly and softly; he tills and plants the ground; sows and waters it joyfully."[4] Together, they struck a remarkable balance. "Luther gave energy to Melanchthon, Melanchthon moderated Luther. They were like substances in a state of positive and negative electricity, which mutually act upon each other."[5] They formed like Voltron to become a mega-Reformer.[6] "These were the leaders of the Wittenberg phalanx."[7]

They were called to Leipsic for the debate. At first, it was to be Eck versus Carlstadt. But the pro-

---

[1] Bainton, *Here I Stand*, 95.
[2] Wylie, *History*, 1.274.
[3] Ibid., 1.299.
[4] Ibid.
[5] d'Aubigné, *History*, 1.361.
[6] Were they to form a hip hop super-duo their album would no doubt be called *Luthanchthon*.
[7] Bainton, *Here I Stand*, 96.

fessors travel together. Luther is itching to enter the fray. The topic of debate for Eck and Carlstadt is the sovereignty of God in salvation, or, the depraved nature of man. Carlstadt was getting wrecked[1] by Eck, who was a homiletical master. Eck loved the heat of battle. "The truth might fare better," said Melanchthon, "at a lower temperature."[2] He was one cool cat. If Huss was heated, Philip was ice cold. "The calm Melanchthon easily detected the weak points of the discussion... If Carlstadt tottered he would whisper a word or slip him a piece of paper with the answer."[3]

Eventually, Duke George allowed Luther into the ring. "Now, my dear Eck," he said, "be brave, and gird thy sword upon thy thigh, thou mighty man!"[4] They enter, as gladiators into the arena, and now Luther begins to shine. "New convictions had sunk deep into his soul; they were not as yet arranged in a system; but in the heat of combat they flashed forth like lightning."[5] Eck was astonished at his knowledge. "The nearer the discussion approached the primitive ages of the Church, the greater was Luther's strength."[6] As to the most primitive source

---

[1] #rekt.

[2] Bainton, *Here I Stand*, 102.

[3] d'Aubigné, *History*, 2.48.

[4] Ibid., 2.30.

[5] Ibid., 2.52.

[6] Ibid., 2.54.

of all, he had "Scripture at his fingers' ends."[1] They debated the legitimacy of the papacy itself, and Luther overthrew the gladiator. It was Eck-zactly as Rome had feared. In the debate hall, Eck's chairs had borne "the insigne of the dragon killer, St. George."[2] He was indeed the dragon killer, but it was the Roman Leviathan which fell under the defeat of its sworn protector.

When it became clear that Eck was facing a fair knock out, he got desperate. He called Luther—wait for it—*a Wicliffite and a Hussite*. "Those odious names," says the chronicler.[3] "The terrors of such an accusation, we in this age can but faintly realize."[4] At their mention "an almost general murmur ran around the hall."[5] These were fighting words. The Hussite wars still resounded in the memories of men, and they were looked upon with ultimate distain in Germany.

The meeting broke for lunch. "Luther availed himself of the interlude to go to the university library and read the acts of the Council of Constance, by which Hus had been condemned."[6] His hungry mind was in continual motion, and drew all that he en-

---

[1] So says an eyewitness. Bainton, *Here I Stand*, 102.

[2] Ibid., 101.

[3] d'Aubigné, *History*, 2.58.

[4] Wylie, *History*, 1.298.

[5] d'Aubigné, *History*, 2.58.

[6] Bainton, *Here I Stand*, 105.

countered within its sphere. Truth was his bread. Astonished at the truths wielded by Huss, he returned to the debate with fresh fire. Afterwards, Eck said, "At any rate, no one is hailing me as the Saxon Hus."[1] True indeed, for he was not worthy of such a noble name.

At the end of the day, "Leipsic allowed the Reformers to see how deep the rift actually was."[2] Luther returned at the head of the train to Wittenberg, to forge mightier weapons.

1520

It is now that the Iron Pen really begins to sing. A torrent of writings rushed out of Wittenberg in this blessed year. The Reformer is at work with miraculous industry. Not only does his theology advance under the strain of battle, but his German does as well. "It is impossible to translate his energetic style, and the strength of that language which grew, so to speak, under his pen, as he wrote."[3] It seems almost worth the *Anfechtungen* of learning German just to read Luther in his native pen strokes.

---

[1] Ibid., 110.

[2] Wylie, *History*, 1.292.

[3] d'Aubigné, *History*, 1.320.

He wrote three books of distinction this year, known as the *Three Treatises*. They are: *To the Christian Nobility in Germany, The Babylonian Captivity of the Church,* and *The Freedom of a Christian.* In them he waxed warm, as he expected the excommunication any day. "They have nothing at all of Christ except the name," he said.[1] "The pope has as little power to command [celibacy] as he has to forbid eating, drinking, the natural movement of the bowels, or growing fat."[2] He was growing in strength. "I shall be called a Wicliffite and a heretic by six hundred names. But what of it?... The only way in which they can prove their opinions and disprove contrary ones is just by saying: that is Wicliffite, Hussite, heretical! They carry this feeble argument always on the tip of their tongues, and they have nothing else."[3] The mantra of our own day is *everyone who disagrees with me is a racist.* There is nothing new under the sun.

The battles had an improving effect on Luther's understanding. "Whether I wish it or not, I am compelled to become more learned every day."[4] The notorious forgery, *The Donation of Constantine,* still held the minds of men captive at this time. It was now that Luther unearthed the fraud. "The time to

---

[1] Luther, *Three Treatises*, 25.
[2] Ibid., 68.
[3] Ibid., 144, 46.
[4] Ibid., 123.

be silent is passed, the time to speak is here. At last, we must unveil the mysteries of Antichrist."[1]

In his work to the nobility, he said, "I know a little song about Rome and the Romanists. If their ears are itching to hear it, I will sing that one to them, too—and I will pitch it in the highest key!"[2] He was speaking of his other book, *The Babylonian Captivity*, which decimated the papal fortress. In it, "Luther had prepared a mine, the explosion of which shook the edifice of Rome to its lowest foundations."[3] It is easy enough to call the pope Antichrist in 2017; it was quite another matter for Martin Luther to do it in 1520. It was bravery incarnate. Not even his German beer could steel him so hardily; the living God was his shield.

It was now that he read the writings of John Huss. "He there found, to his great surprise, the doctrine of St. Paul and of St. Augustine,—that doctrine at which he himself had arrived after so many struggles."[4] He was astonished. "We have all, Paul, Augustine, and myself, been Hussites without knowing it! … God will surely visit it upon the world that the truth was preached to it a century ago, and burned!"[5]

---

[1] d'Aubigné, *History*, 2.95.
[2] Luther, *Three Treatises*, 111.
[3] d'Aubigné, *History*, 2.122.
[4] Ibid., 2.68-9.
[5] Wylie, *History*, 1.305.

The Reformer, with a giant's strength, was
leveling the citadel… Month after month,
rather week by week, he launched treatise on
treatise. The productions of his pen, "like
sparks from under the hammer, each brighter
than that which preceded it," added fresh
force to the conflagration that was blazing on
all sides. His enemies attacked him: they but
drew upon themselves heavier blows.[1]

And now arrived the long-expected document,
the papal bull. Leo threatened excommunication and
called for the burning of Luther's works. What shall
be his response? "To burn books is so easy a matter
that even children can do it… Besides, let them destroy my works! I desire nothing better; for all my
wish has been to lead souls to the Bible, so that they
might afterwards neglect my writings. Great God! If
we had a knowledge of Scripture, what need would
there be of any books of mine?"[2] He went on, "Bulls
neither console nor alarm me. My strength and my
consolation are in a place where neither man nor
devils can reach them."[3] The matter was clearer than
ever before: "This bull condemns Christ himself… I

[1] Ibid.
[2] d'Aubigné, History, 2.143-44.
[3] Ibid., 2.144.

feel much freer now that I am certain the pope is Antichrist."[1] The long-awaited swan is singing, and at a high pitch. The rugged beauty of the song has been well worth the wait.

The bull was published throughout Germany by Eck and Aleander, "which each undertook at the risk of his life."[2] There were fires indeed, but of a different sort than Leo intended. At a university in Louvain, the professors lit a fire in town and called the students and citizens to come burn Luther's books in obedience to the papal summons. And, to their joy, the students, filled with great zeal, walk to the fire with arms full of books and commit them to the flames. It was only afterwards that the professors realized the students had been burning the Roman scholastic works instead of Luther's.[3]

This sealed the break with Rome. "He burnt his ships upon the beach, thus imposing on himself the necessity of advancing and of combating."[4] It had to be done. "It is hard to dissent from all the pontiffs and princes, but there is no other way to escape hell and the wrath of God."[5] What will he do with this bull which calls for the burning of all his books? "So far I have merely fooled with this business of the

---

[1] "Whoever wrote this bull, he is Antichrist." Bainton, *Here I Stand*, 154, 55.

[2] Ibid., 151.

[3] Ibid., 152.

[4] d'Aubigné, *History*, 2.151.

[5] Bainton, *Here I Stand*, 155.

pope."[1] He was not afraid to grow, so sincere was he in his convictions. His mind expanded with every revolution of thought. His foes told him to recant. Lo! he was *always* recanting! "I was wrong, I admit it, when I said that indulgences were 'the pious defrauding of the faithful.' I recant and I say, 'Indulgences are the most impious frauds and imposters of the most rascally pontiffs.'"[2]

At last he *lighted* upon the answer. On the morning of December 10th, a train of students followed him outside of Wittenberg to watch him burn the papal bull of the self-appointed vicar of Christ, along with the sacred canon law. "At the east gate of the city he lit up a fire that has been burning now for three centuries."[3] *Five*, now. "It is evident to all believers that Doctor Luther is an angel of the living God, called to feed Christ's wandering sheep with the word of God. This remark comes from a student who sat under his shocking lectures after he burned the bull."[4] They said he was too harsh. "Alas! Would that I could speak against it with the voice of thunder, and that each of my words was a thunderbolt!"[5] Thor who? All of Germany was on fire. His opponents began to reflect that nothing was actually

---

[1] Ibid., 160.
[2] Ibid., 159.
[3] d'Aubigné, *History*, 2.152.
[4] Ibid., 2.151-52.
[5] Ibid., 2.152.

accomplished by burning his books; the books had been written on the hearts of the people! To destroy *these* writings, all of Germany must be wiped off the earth.

The iron pen flexed its uncanny pith against Rome. "Let it excommunicate and burn my writings! … Let it slay me! … It shall not check that which is advancing. Some great portent is at our doors. I burnt the bull, at first with great trembling, but now I experience more joy from it than from any action I have ever done in my life."[1] The monk excommunicated the pontifical majesty. "Christ will judge whose excommunication will stand."[2] To oppose him was to oppose Christ. How could he be so clear? Because the gospel *is* that clear. He rose up, as it were, a prophet in his own day, not speaking new revelations, but speaking very old ones once again. "To your face, most holy Vicar of God, I say freely that all the condemned articles of John Hus are evangelical and Christian, and yours are downright impious and diabolical."[3]

"His exhortations were heard everywhere. His letters rapidly followed each other. Three presses were constantly occupied in multiplying his writings.

---

[1] Ibid., 2.154.
[2] "As they excommunicated me for the sacrilege of heresy, so I excommunicate them in the name of the sacred truth of God." Bainton, *Here I Stand*, 157.
[3] Ibid., 159.

His words ran through the people."[1] He said at this time, "I am not master of myself; I am carried away by mysterious impulses."[2] Luther is a man on fire. Mastered by truth, he became almost *instinctive*. God's word rushed out of him. He snatched the bolt that Rome had flung at him out of midair and threw it right back at them. Even Frederick defended his actions to Emperor Charles: "If now he has given tit for tat, I hope that His Imperial Majesty will graciously overlook it."[3] Two ages collide in the burning of the bull; it was an epoch. "If eras can be dated," says one, "modern history began on December 10th, 1520."[4]

1521

New players now enter the stage. Emperor Maximillian has died; a new ruler is seated on the throne. Charles became emperor at the age of 19. Two figures, once again, stand before us, in direct contrast. A king and a monk, and yet their destinies were to be reversed before the end.

Charles was a great champion of the papacy. As such, he was now "thrown into collision with a

---

[1] d'Aubigné, *History*, 2.176.

[2] Ibid., 2.176-77.

[3] Bainton, *Here I Stand*, 161.

[4] Lindsay, *History*, 1.252.

power he can neither see nor comprehend."[1] He was dealing with men who communed with the unseen. What could he do to them? He faced a force that was invisible; he was soon to discover that it was also *invincible*. No intrigue of devil nor sword of man can touch it; God was walking among men.

At this time we might expect the Lord to cripple the enemy for final overthrow. What rather happened was that he strengthened him sevenfold. He raised up Charles with all the forces of Rome to flex with all their might against one little monk. God could have given the Reformation to us on a silver platter, but it would be unrecognizable. "The Reformation without martyrs, without scaffolds, without blood! We should hardly have known it. It would be the Reformation without glory and without power."[2]

There was a diet at Worms for Emperor Charles to deal with Luther. His presence was feared by Rome. Tetzel had vanished into hiding after his defeat, but before Worms he seemed to peak his head out of obscurity to say, in the eloquence of Gandalf, *Fly, you fools!* "It is the devil who urges them to this contest," were the words.[3] Others did not desire "to win any more *victories* of the sort that Eck so loudly boasted."[4] Rome knew there was one thing that can-

---

[1] Wylie, *History*, 1.302.
[2] Ibid., 1.304-05.
[3] d'Aubigné, *History*, 2.34.
[4] Wylie, *History*, 1.321.

not come to pass: Luther at Worms. "A dead man returning from the other world and appearing in the midst of the diet, would have been less alarming to the nuncios, the monks, and all the papal host, than the presence of the Wittenberg doctor."[1]

Rome sought his condemnation *in absentia*; Providence sought his appearance. Even some of his sworn enemies stood up and defended his right to be tried in person. Rome had overstepped its bounds one thousand times too many. God whistled for a bee from Wittenberg; he summoned a colorfully plumaged eagle to descend upon Worms.

Luther was now called. He was given a triple safe conduct from the emperor, Frederick, and Duke George. All men expected, notwithstanding such "fayre promises,"[2] that he would die in Worms. But he had become a myth, a legend, *an idea*. "Some would like to crucify him," said one, "and I think that he will not escape; only it is to be feared that he will rise again the third day."[3] He bid farewell to Melanchthon at Wittenberg. "If you survive, my death will be of little consequence."[4] Now that, my dear reader, is discipleship. The entire movement

---

[1] d'Aubigné, *History*, 2.193.
[2] John Foxe, quoted in Luke Walker, *John Huss: The Goose* (Columbus: Wrath and Grace, 2017), 21.
[3] d'Aubigné, *History*, 2.196.
[4] Ibid., 2.220.

had been birthed in Melanchthon; it was no matter if he died. Luther himself was now expendable.

Everyone told him, "You will be burned like Huss!" He said, "Though they should kindle a fire all the way from Worms to Wittenberg, the flames of which reach to heaven, I will walk through it in the name of the Lord,—I would appear before them,— I would enter the jaws of this Behemoth, and break his teeth, confessing the Lord Jesus Christ."[1] He said to another, "Go tell your master, that even should there be as many devils in Worms as tiles on the housetops, still I would enter it!"[2] What manner of man is this? We feel that it is no mere man speaking. Indeed, it is the Lord Jesus Christ that we meet with in these words, taking up a lively residence in one of his servants in an hour of great need. May he do so yet again in striking manner, when such an hour comes once more.

He was walking in the inheritance of the children of God, who receive mighty grace when they need it, and not a moment sooner. Reflecting at his death, he said, "I was then undaunted. I feared nothing. God can indeed render a man intrepid at any time."[3] Simple faith in Christ was his shield. "The man who, when he is attacked by the enemy, protects himself

---

[1] Ibid., 2.226.
[2] Ibid., 2.230.
[3] Ibid.

with the shield of faith, is like Perseus, with the Gorgon's head. Whoever looked at it fell dead. In like manner should we present the Son of God to the snares of the devil."[1]

He appeared before the diet the first day, and about thirty or so books of his are laid out before him. "Are these your books?" He was about to answer, but his conscience checked him; he had better make sure that they were really his own! All the titles were read; yes indeed, they are Luther's. Only one more question did they pose to him: "Do you recant what is written in these?" The moment is upon him; every breath is stilled in anticipation. And Luther asked for time.

Was he second guessing what he had believed and preached for so long? It seems that it was rather wisdom and care that animated him at this juncture. He wished to make sure that he knew exactly how he would answer. Paul himself was among the Corinthians with fear and trembling; and yet, it was not a faithless cowardice that animated that ancient preacher. The diet granted him one day.

He returned to his quarters, woke up early the next morning, and wrestled with God in prayer. It seems that one of his friends sat outside and recorded some of what was said for posterity. In

---

[1] Ibid., 2.241-42.

prayer, he knew his weakness, he trembled before what he was called to do, he expected death, and yet he called upon God with faith to help him. God, the mighty fortress and ever present help in time of trouble, heard his servant, and answered with decided power.

He spoke that day in such a way that those who were present said, "He was more than himself."[1] Yea, there was a Greater than Luther in their midst:

> I have written works on many different subjects. There are some in which I have treated of faith and good works, in a manner at once so pure, so simple, and so scriptural, that even my adversaries, far from finding anything to censure in them, allow that these works are useful, and worthy of being read by all pious men. The papal bull, however violent it may be, acknowledges this. If, therefore, I were to retract these, what should I do?[2]

He reasoned thus with the diet. "The chancellor...rose and demanded his answer. What a moment! The fate of ages hangs on it. The emperor leans forward, the princes sit motionless, the very

---

[1] Wylie, *History*, 1.339.

[2] d'Aubigné, *History*, 2.245.

guards are still: all eager to catch the first utterances of the monk."[1] Let us hear it from Luther's own mouth:

> I cannot submit my faith either to the Pope or to the Councils, because it is clear as day they have frequently erred and contradicted each other. Unless, therefore, I am convinced by the testimony of Scripture, or on plain and clear grounds of reason, so that conscience shall bind me to make acknowledgment of error, *I can and will not retract*, for it is neither safe nor wise to do anything contrary to conscience.[2]

And then these words, which yet echo through time:

> *HERE I STAND. I CAN DO NO OTHER. MAY GOD HELP ME. AMEN.*[3]

"Words which still thrill our hearts at an interval of [five] centuries. Thus spoke a monk before the emperor and the mighty ones of the nation."[4] The assembly was stunned! At this moment, the two most powerful forces on the earth are singing at their

---

[1] Wylie, *History*, 1.340-41.
[2] Ibid., 1.344.
[3] Ibid.
[4] d'Aubigné, *History*, 2.249.

highest pitch: the word of God, and the conscience of man, as one poor monk defies the world and stands for truth.

That night Duke Eric of Brunswick sent him a pitcher of Einbeck beer. "My master," said the footman servant, "invites you to refresh yourself with this draught."[1] Luther imbibed to God's glory and uttered a blessing upon the noble duke: "As this day Duke Eric has remembered me, so may the Lord Jesus Christ remember him in the hour of his last struggle."[2] That duke, when he was on his death bed, called his servant to open up the Scriptures and read to him. The servant randomly opened a page and lighted on these words: "Truly, I say to you, whoever gives you a cup of water to drink because you belong to Christ will be no means lose his reward."[3] The blessing had returned on the duke's head as he passed into eternity, rejoicing in the hope of eternal life. Luther had many true friends, though the powers that be were marshalled as one against him. God has his knights in play as well as his bishops.

He wrote letters to inform his friends of what had passed. "I thought his majesty would have assembled some fifty doctors at Worms to convict the monk outright. But not at all.—Are these your

[1] Wylie, *History*, 1.345.
[2] Ibid.
[3] Mark 9:41.

books?—Yes!—Will you retract them?—No!—
Well, then, be gone!—There is the whole history."[1]

Charles rashly let Luther go, but regretted it to
the bitter end. He died in a monastery, saying these
words: "I confess that I committed a great fault by
permitting Luther to live."[2] Thus passed the emperor
as a monk, while the monk lived on as a king among
men, even unto eternity, reigning with Christ. How
the tables had mightily turned.

Before quitting Worms, Luther sent letters back
home. Among them dwells an enigmatic little word:
"A little while and you shall not see me; and after a
little while and you shall see me."[3] He travelled the
road back to Wittenberg, rejoicing in the help God
had granted him. But several days into the journey,
suddenly his carriage is surrounded by armed and
masked men upon horseback. They pin down his
driver and snatch Luther. They threw a bag over his
head, put him on a horse, and "in the twinkling of an
eye vanished into the gloomy forest."[4] Luther is
gone.

TO BE CONTINUED…

---

[1] d'Aubigné, *History*, 2.269.
[2] Ibid., 2.254.
[3] Ibid., 2.270.
[4] Ibid., 2.276.

*Strangely have the scenes been shifted, and the
stage has become suddenly dark. A moment ago,
the theatre was crowded with great actors, powerful
interests were in conflict, and mighty issues were
about to be decided. All at once, the action is
arrested. The brilliant throng vanishes, and deep
silence succeeds the tumult and noise. And we
have time to meditate on what we have seen, to
revolve its lessons, and to feel in our hears the
presence and the hand of that great Ruler who sits
king upon the floods.*[1]

---

[1] Wylie, *History*, 1.349.

78287596R00040

Made in the USA
Columbia, SC
14 October 2017